TARGET : FALKIRK

Falkirk District
in the
Second World War

John Walker

Falkirk Council Community Services

FOREWORD

There have been few events in recent history that have exercised such a major influence on the everyday lives of ordinary people as the Second World War. Many of our older citizens have vivid memories of rationing, air raid shelters and even the occasional air raid. There are many publications available charting the progress of the war but, until now, none describing what daily life was like in the Falkirk area for our parents and grandparents during this time.

This new book, written by local historian John Walker, describes the effect of this momentous period on the ordinary people of this area.

I would like to thank John Walker for writing this absorbing book and Anna Herron and John Dickson of Library Services for editing and publishing it. I am sure it will prove a useful resource for all those interested in the Second World War and for all those who lived in the Falkirk area during those years.

Stephen Dunlop,
Director,
Community Services,
Falkirk Council.

ISBN : 0906586 925

Published by : Falkirk Council Library Services

Year of Publication : 2001

Code : 251

ACKNOWLEDGEMENTS

Firstly, I would like to extend my thanks to Geoff Bailey and Ian Scott, who have acted as editors, picture finders, trackers-down of good anecdotes and proof-readers, and have been as generous as ever with comments and suggestions. Geoff has also acted as liaison with staff at Falkirk Library Services and with the Royal Commission on the Ancient and Historic Monuments of Scotland.

There have also been many other contributors. My mother and father, Helen and George Walker, both lived in the town for most of the period and have a fund of stories which add colour to what is, for those of us from the post-war generations, a rather grey period. The late Mr W. Berwick provided much of the material on the Home Guard. The Committee of the Polish Ex-Servicemen's Club in Falkirk was kind enough to spend what was for me a highly enjoyable evening reminiscing about their wartime experiences. Several of my fellow members of Falkirk Local History Society, particularly John Reid and Brian Watters, supplied useful material. Thanks are also due to Douglas Carr, former editor of the Falkirk Herald.

As work on the book progressed I made several appeals for information in the local press, each of which generated a substantial response. I think I have been able to reply to everyone who contacted me but if I have missed anyone I hope they will accept my apologies and thanks.

A note about the photographs. The majority come from the Falkirk Museums collection, the Falkirk Herald or the Royal Commission on the Ancient and Historic Monuments of Scotland and I would like to extend my appreciation to each of these organisations. Any photograph or graphic not otherwise credited was taken by me.

A number of my friends and former colleagues at what was then called Zeneca Grangemouth were kind enough to proof read early drafts of the text and suggest improvements. It is much the better for their efforts.

My wife Rhona has once again had to live with yet another history project. At least she knows where to find me!

Finally, both Andrew Euan Walker and Mark Henry James Bailey arrived on the scene while their respective fathers were working on this book and it is dedicated to them.

John Walker,
Bainsford,
March 2001

CONTENTS

THE GATHERING STORM

In the early morning of Friday, September 1st 1939, the German army, navy and air force launched an assault of unprecedented ferocity across their eastern border into Poland. The Polish armed forces, although extremely courageous, were no match for the Germans who advanced quickly towards the Polish capital city, Warsaw.

Some months previously, in April 1939, Great Britain and France had guaranteed to come to Poland's aid if she was attacked and Germany was therefore given a deadline to withdraw her forces to their own territory or risk a wider European war. The German government chose not to heed this warning, safe in the knowledge that a nonaggression pact signed with the Soviet Union only the week before would guarantee no interference from the Russians. Other than issue threats, there was little Britain and France could actually do.

As a consequence the British Prime Minister Neville Chamberlain broadcast to the country at lunchtime on Sunday, September 3rd:

> *"This morning the British Ambassador in Berlin handed the German government a final note stating that, unless we heard from them by 11 o'clock that they were prepared, at once, to withdraw their troops from Poland, a state of war would exist between us. I have to tell you now that no such undertaking has been received and that, consequently, this country is at war with Germany."*

A mere 20 years and 10 months after the Armistice which brought an end to the fighting in "The War to end all Wars", Europe was once again plunged into conflict.

The outbreak of war came as no surprise to the British government. As long ago as 1933, the same year that Adolf Hitler had become Chancellor of Germany, plans had been laid for a programme of rearmament. The Government had believed that war with Germany was inevitable and that it would probably happen before the end of the 1930s. Its plans had, therefore, been laid on the basis of having the British armed forces brought to the highest possible state of preparedness by the summer of 1939. So accurate were the British predictions that, for example, when war was declared almost all of the Royal Navy's capital ships had been extensively modernised or were entirely new. Two of the ships which had not been modernised were HMS Hood and HMS Royal Oak, both of which would be sunk early in the conflict.

The destruction of the Royal Oak on October 14th 1939, in the supposedly safe anchorage of Scapa Flow in the Orkney Islands, was nonetheless a particularly bitter blow to morale. A German submarine penetrated the defences to send the battleship to the bottom, where she remains to this day. Four men from the district died in the attack: Stoker James Sorley from Weir Street, Falkirk; Marine John Stevenson from Lime Road, Camelon; Telegraphist Ellis Wilcock, originally from James Street, Stenhousemuir and Seaman Edward Barker from Binniehill, Slamannan.

Stoker James Sorley, Marine John Stevenson and Seaman Edward Barker *Falkirk Herald*

Hitler had also been convinced that war was inevitable but he had not believed that it would break out before the early 1940s. Consequently the German armaments programme had not reached full capacity when hostilities commenced, a factor that would influence the course of the war as it was experienced in and around Falkirk.

"The Bomber Will Always Get Through"

The First World War had been predominately a land war. Huge numbers of soldiers on each side died trying to take a few extra yards of territory on a front line that remained essentially static for nearly three years. Although many soldiers from the Falkirk area were lost in the Great War, the fighting was done far away. Scotland had only limited first hand experience of the war, with the occasional shelling of the east coast by ships of the German navy and one raid on Edinburgh by a German airship. There were, however, some signs that the next war would be fought differently.

Perhaps the most important military development in the period between the First and Second World Wars was the rise in the capability of combat aircraft, particularly bombers. The German Air Force in the First World War had been able to mount raids against London and other towns in the south of England using their famous Gotha bombers from bases in France. The Royal Air Force had been preparing for its first night raid on Berlin the very day the Armistice, which brought hostilities to an end, came into force. To some military thinkers it was becoming obvious that air power, and particularly the bomber, would be the strategic key to winning any future war. Some influential sections of the British government believed that there was no effective defence against bombers and the only way for a country to protect itself was to build even more of them than a potential enemy. The "Trenchard Doctrine" as this theory was known, after Viscount Trenchard, founder of the RAF and a fervent believer in the invincibility of the bomber, underpinned British defence policy for much of the 1920s and 1930s.

There was in fact some justification for these beliefs. The Spanish Civil War, fought between 1936 and 1939, had seen fearful damage wrought by the German and Italian air force elements of General Franco's Nationalist forces. Similarly, the war between China and Japan, which broke out in 1931 and would continue until the defeat of Japan in 1945, had seen several Chinese cities devastated by aerial attack, thus seeming to prove Stanley Baldwin's famous 1932 prediction that "the bomber will always get through".

As a result there was a widespread expectation that within minutes of war being declared British skies would be darkened by fleets of German bombers flying in to attack targets the length and breadth of the country. Central Scotland would be an obvious choice for such raids; not only were there important military targets like Rosyth naval base and several airfields, there were also industries such as shipbuilding and engineering, which would be critical to the British war effort. The Falkirk area with its iron foundries, which would soon be turning out vast quantities of munitions, the important docks and large new airfield at Grangemouth, could surely expect to be visited by hostile aircraft early in the conflict. For all these reasons defence against attack from the air and dealing with the aftermath of such attacks was the first priority of all the responsible authorities, from national government to town and county councils.

Preparations for War

The Declaration of War brought a number of emergency regulations into immediate effect. Everyone had to carry their gas mask and national identity card, and blackout regulations were enforced. The blackout was designed to prevent enemy aircraft from using any lights on the ground to assist with their navigation. All windows had to be made lightproof, street lights were extinguished and vehicle lights were shrouded. Falkirk Town Council even discussed the benefits of painting the glass panels in their greenhouses, to prevent reflection! They eventually decided against this course of action. There were of course many accidents, some of them fatal. At least one person was killed in Falkirk by a motor vehicle whose dimmed lights they had not seen, and it seems that it was not uncommon to find yourself trying to get into the wrong house in the darkness.

It is questionable exactly how effective the blackout in Falkirk district was, given the many foundries with their furnaces and glowing spoil heaps. Any moonlight or starlight would also make the Rivers Forth, Carron and Avon and the canals stand out against the black background, with the docks at Grangemouth being particularly conspicuous. Robert Porteous, in his book "Grangemouth's Modern History", notes that on one occasion when a stray German bomber did fly over the town, most of the citizens threw open their doors to see what was making all the noise!

On the whole, though, blackout regulations appear to have been followed as closely as possible, which is just as well since penalties were quickly and heavily enforced. On the first Monday in November 1939 Falkirk Sheriff Court heard the cases of 18 cyclists, 8 householders, 2 shopkeepers and an open-air trader for breaches of the blackout. The cyclists were all charged with having inadequately screened and dimmed front or rear lights. They were fined 5 shillings, with the alternative of 5 days in prison. The householders were fined between 5 and 10 shillings each, with a custodial alternative. The shopkeepers were both chip shop proprietors. One, from Larbert, was fined 30 shillings with an alternative of 10 days while the other from Falkirk was fined 10 shillings with an alternative of 7 days. The open-air trader was found to have had an outdoor wood fire. He claimed to have extinguished it, but that the wind must have reignited the embers. He was fined 30 shillings with an alternative of 10 days.

Another emergency regulation banned meetings of more than 10 people at any location. This meant that theatre, cinema and sports events were all cancelled. The regulation also made it impossible to hold football games. Falkirk Football Club players reported for training on Monday 4th September, to be told of the regulations by their manager. He advised them to find other jobs for the duration of the war, advice promptly taken by star player Kenny Dawson, who joined the local Auxiliary Fire Service. Cinemas and theatres also had to close. These regulations were, however, withdrawn very quickly when the government came to accept that the benefit to morale of leaving these entertainments in place far outweighed any potential dangers.

Schools were not allowed to open on September 4th unless they had adequate air raid shelter provision. Stirling County Council had been working for some weeks to build shelters at all its schools and by the beginning of October only Falkirk Technical (Graeme High) and Comely Park Schools were awaiting completion of the work. Some schools did not need purpose built shelters as they already had buildings that could be pressed into service.

On the more general provision of air raid shelters, things did not go quite so well. There were two separate issues the local councils needed to address - the provision of individual domestic shelters and larger public shelters. Home owners had to make their own arrangements and the Falkirk Herald published a sketch showing how a shelter could be constructed using timber, corrugated iron and sandbags. Sandbags were in plentiful supply, being filled at the sand quarry in Bell's Meadow.

Building an air raid shelter in the grounds of Falkirk High School, 1939
Falkirk Herald

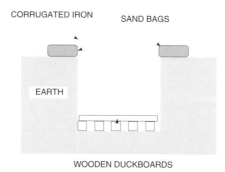

CORRUGATED IRON   SAND BAGS

EARTH

WOODEN DUCKBOARDS

Sketch of Falkirk Herald's design for an air raid shelter trench
Author

Local housing authorities, either the various burgh councils or Stirling County Council, were responsible for providing shelters for their tenants. Their efforts appear to have been concentrated at first on the famous Anderson Shelter. This was a pre-fabricated corrugated iron structure that was bolted together and buried in a trench for about half its height. The part of the shelter remaining above ground was then covered with earth and turf. Anderson sections could be fitted together to make larger shelters if required.

One place where the Anderson was not a success was Grangemouth. Grange-mouth Town Council acquired a substantial stock and began distributing them. However the Anderson needed a trench at least three feet deep and, because Grangemouth is so low-lying, almost any hole in the ground of more than a few inches depth immediately filled with water. Grangemouth's air raid shelters had to be built above ground!

By early 1941 Falkirk Town Council had started to build more substantial brick air raid shelters in the gardens of its properties. The council adopted two distinct designs. The first, and much more common, was built on a rectangular plan with a door at one end of the longest face and a flat concrete roof. These are still fairly easy to find today. The second type is less common and was of a square plan with a pitched roof and a door in the gable wall. Both types were built with a brick blast wall a few feet in front of the door and a specially weak-ened section of one wall. This was designed to blow out in the event of a near miss and prevent the blast knocking the shelter down. Internal furnishings were left up to the occupiers, but cot beds and a small stove were usual.

A surviving domestic air raid shelter, Bainsford
Author

The matter of public shelters was less straightforward, at least in Falkirk. At the outbreak of war little had been done but the council eventually started work on a number of shelters, including one in Newmarket Street Gardens, in October, pointing out that they had not been told how the building work was to be paid for. Even when they were completed there was still controversy with the Falkirk Herald taking the Council to task for insisting on keeping the public shelters locked until they were needed!

Gas! Gas! Gas!

There remained the abiding fear that, if the German air force attacked, they might be dropping more than just high explosive bombs. Both the British and German governments had a fear of chemical weapons which was founded on the experiences of troops in the First World War. The Germans had begun using chlorine gas as a weapon, which of course brought about British reprisals. At first the gas was released from cylinders, but this could result in the gas blowing back over friendly territory if the wind changed direction. To overcome this

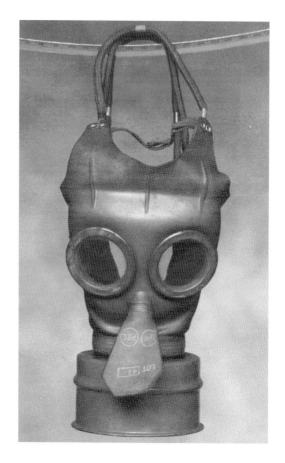

A typical civilian pattern gas mask
Falkirk Museums Service

problem artillery shells were produced which had gas instead of explosive warheads.

The Germans kept up their research into chemical weapons throughout the First World War, developing a series of liquids and gases. Their most useful discovery, from a weapons point of view, was a corrosive liquid that came to be known as mustard gas because of its strong and characteristic smell. This name was slightly misleading since the substance was actually a liquid which caused a blistering of the skin, difficulty in breathing, blindness and ultimately death. Its corrosive nature meant that it would penetrate clothing and it would also stay active in the environment for a considerable time after being deployed, making ground or equipment that had been exposed unusable without decontamination.

Such was the international revulsion at the effects of chemical warfare that the use of chemical and biological agents was banned by the Geneva Protocol of 1925. However, both Britain and Germany retained the means to manufacture, stockpile and deliver chemical weapons if they so chose. Given the awareness in Britain that the Germans had a chemical warfare capability, it became necessary to devise a strategy to defend against its use.

Civilian gas masks had been stockpiled for some time and were distributed to the public through the Air Raid Precautions network. The main locations in the town of Falkirk were the High School (now Woodlands High School), the ARP headquarters in Weir Street and their store in West Bridge Street. Special gas masks for children were manufactured in red and blue rubber, while babies would be put in a respirator cot. This had a cast iron base and a gastight cover, into which air was pumped through a filter. There were even gas masks for horses.

For the gas mask to be of any use there had to be some form of early warning of a gas attack. The air raid warning siren would sound if there were enemy aircraft in the vicinity. In order to establish if gas was being used a number of boards painted with a special chemically sensitive coating were set up around the district. This coating was a greenish yellow in appearance and it would change colour in the presence of certain chemicals. If this happened the air raid wardens would put on their gas masks and would use a special rattle, similar to those which used to be common at football matches, to warn of the presence of gas. This was the instruction to don your mask.

While the gas mask might help you to breathe, it was also necessary to decontaminate yourself if a substance like mustard gas got on your skin or clothes. Falkirk Town Council issued explicit instructions:

> *"In the event of a person being splashed with liquid gas, remove any contaminated clothing and have a bath at once. If liquid gas is observed on the skin, and if you have any bleach ointment, apply a little, provided not more than a few minutes have elapsed since the occurrence. Be careful with your own hands. Remember to burn the cloth used for removing the liquid gas. Do not keep gas contaminated clothing inside your house. Report all the circumstances immediately to your warden, who will advise you what to do and make the necessary arrangements for you. In the event of becoming contaminated with liquid gas while out of doors, do not hesitate to remove any contaminated clothing and go as quickly as possible to the public baths in the Pleasance or the Gas Cleansing Centre in Stirling Road, Camelon."*

Purpose built decontamination centres were set up at a variety of locations in the district. These large brick buildings equipped with showers, air filtering plant and stocks of clean clothes, would provide shelter in the case of a gas attack and allow victims to change contaminated clothes and wash any corrosive substances from their bodies. Thankfully, these were precautions that never had to be tested.

Fire

It was widely anticipated that the aftereffects of an air raid would include widespread outbreaks of fire, especially if the bombers were dropping incendiary munitions. Each town had a fire service provided by either the burgh or county council as appropriate, but to reinforce the existing provision AFS stations were established in most areas.

Falkirk AFS was based at a station in Burnbank Road, Bainsford, with direct communication to the burgh fire headquarters in Newmarket Street. By October 1939 the local AFS had 120 men and 9 appliances, most of which were trailer pumps towed around by powerful cars. Falkirk also had access to a launch on the Forth and Clyde Canal that could be used as an emergency fireboat if needed. When not in use it was moored at Bainsford Bridge. A number of enthusiastic

The Gas Decontamination Centre in the Lido, Stenhousemuir
Falkirk Museums Service

cyclists were also employed as messengers. Other AFS stations were located around the district, for example at the council yard in Lime Street, Grangemouth and the Crown Inn Building garage in Stenhousemuir.

Most of the large foundries and other industrial concerns had their own fire fighting equipment that was also made available if needed. The firefighting team at Carrongrove paper mill was especially highly regarded and regularly assisted the Denny fire brigade. The AFS also arranged fire watching teams, which would take turns to man observation posts to spot the first signs of any fire and report it to the control room.

Precautions were also taken against the possibility of an air raid fracturing a main and depriving the fire services of water. In Grangemouth, Bainsford and Bonnybridge there was water available from rivers or from the Forth and Clyde Canal. In other areas, like Falkirk town centre, it was necessary to build large water tanks. One of these was set up at the High Street end of Silver Row.

To provide yet further backup for both the full time and auxiliary fire services the ARP trained its members in fire fighting and rescue techniques. These courses took place at the council depot in Cooperage Lane, behind Brockville football ground. Most of the burghs had specialist rescue teams tasked with

Top : Falkirk AFS at Burnbank Road, Bainsford, around 1940
Bottom : Grangemouth AFS with Engine No. 7
Falkirk Museums Service

locating and removing survivors from bombed buildings. Training for these teams was often provided by the local mines rescue service.

The Casualties of War

Any air raid would almost certainly destroy the houses and personal posses-sions of the civilian population, so to accommodate and feed the homeless in the short term a number of locations were designated as Rest Centres. These were generally schools, which would have the necessary space, washing and cooking facilities. Both primary and secondary schools were   designated as Rest Centres. Should any of the Rest Centres be destroyed, Second Line Rest Centres would be established in other buildings, with less suitable facilities. These were mostly church halls, but in Falkirk the Pavilion Café at 14 High Street was also nominated.

Local hospitals were, of course, expected to deal with serious casualties. Falkirk Infirmary and the Stirling District Mental Hospital (Bellsdyke) evacuated their non-critical patients to allow for the expected influx of casualties, both civilian and military. Plans were also in place to deal with the "walking wounded", who might need first aid treatment but were not so badly injured as to require hospitalisation. Three first aid posts were established in Falkirk, at Dawson Park School, the Gymnasium in Baird Street, Camelon and in a purpose built post in Bells Meadow. Casualties were to be classified as "killed", "seriously wounded" or "slightly wounded". Lists would be published, if possible, at three-hourly intervals and posted at police stations and council offices.

The Rest Centres were intended to provide only temporary shelter. To help homeless people find other accommodation and provide them with new documents or financial assistance, an Information Centre would be opened at Comely Park School. If it proved impossible to go to friends or family, emergency ac-

The First Aid Post in Bell's Meadow, used today by the Air Training Corps
Author

commodation would be arranged by the Billeting Officer. Local families with spare rooms registered with the Billeting Officer and, in return for a Billeting Allowance, they would "put up" the homeless until their houses could be repaired or other arrangements made. The Public Assistance offices and Labour Exchanges also had emergency procedures to deal with people who had no income or had been made unemployed as the result of an air raid.

The Enemy Arrives

In common with all other areas of the country Falkirk district braced itself for the onslaught. But the bombers didn't come, on the first day of the war, or the second. In fact it was over a month before German aircraft were seen in any numbers over the district. It was, as we now know, far beyond the capability of the Luftwaffe at that time to even fly a bomber from Germany to many parts of the British Isles and back again. German military thinking saw the air force primarily as a tactical resource, flying relatively short-range missions in support of ground or naval forces. Germany had in fact given up the development of long-range heavy bombers in 1936, and no new designs would be available until after 1941. The bombers in the Luftwaffe inventory at the beginning of the war were, by British standards, short-ranged and lightly armed.

Even they, however, could reach Scotland including Falkirk when operating from Westerland airfield on the German North Sea island of Sylt. Their first targets were the Royal Navy installations around Scapa Flow in Orkney. These bases were heavily defended by both Royal Navy and RAF fighters, and the Germans suffered losses. The aviation historian David Smith has pointed out that the air battle for Orkney was fought and won long before the events we now call the Battle of Britain had even started.

Although the Falkirk area was visited by high flying reconnaissance   aircraft from the first few days of the war, it was not until Monday October 16th 1939 that more hostile aircraft arrived.   On that day the Luftwaffe mounted a raid on the River Forth with the intention of bombing the battle cruiser HMS Hood, which had been spotted on her way to the naval dockyard at Rosyth. A squadron of Junkers Ju88 bombers, then the most modern design in the German air force, was despatched with orders to sink the Hood, but only if she was still in open water. At that time in the war both the Luftwaffe and the RAF were under orders to avoid damaging civilian targets if at all possible.

The ship the Germans believed to be the Hood was actually HMS Repulse and was by this stage safely in dock, but a number of cruisers and destroyers were spotted in the river near the Forth Bridge, providing tempting targets for the German bombers. The commander of the attacking force, Oberst Helmut Pohle, dived through a barrage of anti-aircraft gunfire to drop his bombs on the ships. It was this sudden heavy gunfire which brought many people in the eastern end of the district outside to see what was going on. They soon had a grandstand view of an aerial battle as Spitfires based at airfields along the Forth caught up with the bombers.

The Germans flew as low as they could in an attempt to escape the fighters, and once it had dropped its bombs the Ju88 was almost as fast as the early Spitfires were. The bombers headed out over the North Sea, all the time with their rear gunners firing continually in an attempt to keep the Spitfires at a safe distance. Colonel Pohle still had a rear gunner, but not a rear gun. His cockpit canopy had been blown off in his bombing attack taking the gun with it. Now defenceless against the Spitfires his aircraft was shot down into the Firth of Forth near Crail, from where the survivors of his crew were rescued by a fishing boat. They were later taken to a military hospital and then to Edinburgh Castle, before being transferred to a prisoner of war camp. The RAF claimed a total of four bombers destroyed in the action, although it seems likely that only two were actually shot down.

This raid has gone down in aviation history. Pohle's aircraft (4D+AK) was the second to be shot down over mainland Britain, but only by 10 minutes! The first had been another member of his squadron, Oberleutnant Sigmund Storp's Ju88 (4D+DH), shot down into the Forth near Port Seton. These were also the first enemy "kills" credited to the Spitfire. The bombers, however, had done serious damage to the destroyer HMS Mohawk, fatally injuring her captain.

After all the effort put into the air raid alarm system, when enemy aircraft actually appeared the sirens didn't work! The population of Edinburgh only realised the aircraft flying over the city were hostile when the defending fighters had opened fire, showering the streets with spent cartridge cases. The Falkirk Herald was indignant, asking where was the point in having an expensive early warning system if something as basic as the air raid sirens could not be relied upon to work. The air raid sirens in Falkirk actually sounded for the first time in December, but only as a test.

A Change of Tactics

In the spring of 1940 the German army launched a swift and highly success-ful attack against Belgium, Holland and France. They squeezed the Allied ar-mies against the northern French coast, where large numbers of soldiers were evacuated from the beaches of Dunkirk. This high-speed advance captured many French airfields and brought the Luftwaffe within range of targets in southern England, paving the way for the events we know today as the Battle of Britain.

Although many of their bombers were moved into the campaign against London, Central Scotland, and particularly the River Forth, was still a target. The Germans, however, realised that daylight missions were becoming too ex-pensive in terms of aircraft and crews lost and from the summer of 1940 they switched to night raids. This resulted in an increase in the numbers of search-lights deployed to spot the raiders and illuminate them for anti-aircraft gunfire.

There were always fighters available to defend the area, often squadrons withdrawn from the front line and sent north for a "rest". From late 1940 onwards there was also a small number of specialist night fighter aircraft avail-able. However these aircraft did not carry radar and were not particularly effec-tive. Indeed the first successful night interception over Scotland was carried out by a Spitfire of No 603 Squadron, which shot down a Heinkel He111 bomber just after 1am in the morning of June 25th 1940. The bomber crashed into the River Forth off Bo'ness.

The raids continued with some loss of life and a great deal of material dam-age. The river was mined and bombs were dropped on land targets. The sea mines claimed several ships including, on November 22nd 1940, the steamship Glen, which blew up while carrying ammunition between Grangemouth and Crombie in Fife.

In the spring of 1941 the Germans launched a series of massed bomber raids against the shipbuilding and engineering industries in Belfast and on the Scot-tish west coast, which culminated in the Clydebank Blitz in March, and other attacks on Clydeside later in the spring. Once again the Falkirk area escaped any determined attack, and such bombing as there was appears to have been the result of aircraft jettisoning their unused bombs on the way back from the Clyde. It was in the March and April 1941 period that most bombs landed in our area, with explosions at Maddiston, Slamannan, High Bonnybridge and around both Grangemouth and Falkirk. An explosion at Slamannan appears to have been caused by a heavy parachute mine rather than a conventional bomb. There was also damage done at the Royal Scottish National Hospital in Larbert, where two bombs landed. Although the local AFS never had to deal with major bomb damage in Falkirk they did provide support for their counterparts on Clydeside during the heavy raids there.

In the summer of 1941 the situation changed once again. Germany invaded her former ally the Soviet Union, and many Luftwaffe units were moved east to take part in these campaigns. Although there were still visits from the Luftwaffe, especially attacks on North Sea shipping and fishing boats, there were few further attacks on the mainland. The RAF gradually went on the offensive against German units in Norway and Denmark, forcing them to switch from offensive to defensive tactics. The last air raid noted against the Scottish mainland was a low level, high-speed night attack by a single aircraft against the Edinburgh area in the summer of 1944.

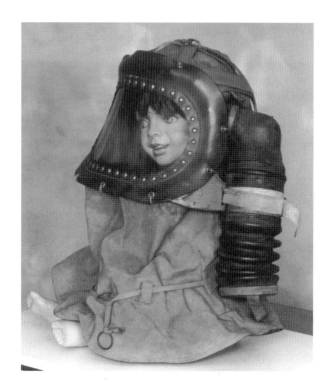

A special gasproof cot for babies and infants
Falkirk Museums Service

THE HOME FRONT

For the people who lived and worked in the Falkirk area during the war life was fraught with difficulties but, at the same time, there were compensations. In contrast with most of the 1930s, and after a slow start, industry was working flat out and anyone not in the armed forces who wanted a job could get one without difficulty. Income tax was high but wages were good. There was rationing of basic foodstuffs, but the generation that grew up during the war years is regarded as the fittest the country has ever seen.

The overwhelming feeling in the first few days of the war was probably one of apprehension as people waited for their towns and villages to be bombarded from the air. In many parts of Falkirk neighbours worked together to dig shelter trenches in gardens and back courts, the majority of which seem to have filled with water almost as soon as they were dug! By the end of the summer of 1940, when it became apparent that invasion was less and less likely, most people seem to have decided to make the best of a bad situation.

"What's a Banana?"

In January 1940 the Government announced plans to ration certain foodstuffs. The reasoning behind this decision was outlined by the Ministry of Food in the leaflet reproduced on page 24. The last paragraph which promised no queues was particularly optimistic - most people who lived through the war remember nothing but queues!

The real reason behind rationing was the memory of the damage done by the German submarine force in the First World War. The Government knew that it was possible that the German navy could mount an extremely effective blockade of Britain with its large fleet of powerful U-boats. This was important because most food came by sea, and the country would be forced to depend on home produced foodstuffs only.

Everyone was issued with a book of ration coupons, which could be exchanged for set amounts of rationed foodstuffs from whichever shop they had registered with. For example in March 1940, when rationing was introduced, each adult was entitled to purchase 1s 10d worth of meat per week. Each child under 11 was entitled to meat to the value of 11d per week. The Ministry was also keen to point out that not all meats were rationed. You could buy unre-

Ministry  of Food

REASONS FOR

RATIONING

War has meant the re-planning of our food supplies. Half our meat and most of our bacon, butter and sugar come from overseas. Here are four reasons for rationing:

1. RATIONING PREVENTS WASTE OF FOOD. We must not ask our sailors to bring us unnecessary food cargoes at the risk of their lives.

2. RATIONING INCREASES OUR WAR EFFORT. Our shipping carries food and armaments in their raw and finished states, and other essential raw materials for home consumption and the export trade. To reduce our purchases of food abroad is to release ships to bring us other imports. So we shall strengthen the war effort.

3. RATIONING DIVIDES SUPPLIES EQUALLY. There will be ample supplies for our 44½ million people, but we must divide them fairly, everyone being treated alike. No one must be left out.

4. RATIONING PREVENTS UNCERTAINTY. Your Ration Book assures you of your fair share. Rationing means that there will be no uncertainty - and no queues.

YOUR RATION BOOK IS YOUR PASSPORT TO EASY PURCHASING OF BACON & HAM, BUTTER AND SUGAR

AN ANNOUNCEMENT BY THE MINISTRY OF FOOD, GT WESTMINSTER HOUSE, LONDON, SW1

stricted amounts of liver, kidney, tripe, heart, ox tail, sausage and meat pies, but only if the sausages and pies contained less than 50% meat. Chicken and game were also "off the ration". Wartime sausages are remembered by many as being so full of breadcrumbs that they burnt almost as soon as they were put into the frying pan. You could save your coupons up if you wanted to buy more food for a special event like a birthday or a wedding.

"Off the ration" didn't mean easily available. Butchers could get limited supplies but it was first come, first served, hence the standard wartime instruction to join any queue you see - there might be something interesting on sale! Most imported fruits were not rationed but remained practically unobtainable because of the small amounts available at any one time. Vegetables were generally available and became the staple of the wartime diet. Any available space was utilised to grow them, even school playing fields. At Falkirk High School an area of ground was dug into vegetable plots, with each plot being shared between two pupils.

In July 1940 the scope of rationing was extended. Tea, which was of course imported, was restricted to two ounces per person per week. Cups of tea in restaurants were not rationed but proprietors had to account for all the tea they used. Margarine and cooking fats were placed on ration and it was decreed that the icing of confectionery was to stop and restaurants were to stop serving both a fish and a meat course in the same meal.

The Ministry was keen to encourage the use of locally grown vegetables to supplement or replace the rarer cuts of meat. For much of the war cookery demonstrations were held in the Gas Showroom in Falkirk High Street. For example, in May 1940 Miss M C Gumpertz MCA of R & A Main, the Camelon based manufacturer of gas catering equipment, gave a lecture in the Showroom on "How attractive and nourishing meals could be cooked in spite of food rationing".

Considerable ingenuity was displayed by local people in making their rations stretch as far as possible. It is possible to find recollections of sponge cakes made with liquid paraffin, which no doubt also served as a useful laxative! Whale steaks were tried at one time, but they were generally regarded as awful. If potatoes were scarce, mashed butter beans could be used instead.

The shortage of sugar meant that it was impossible to make jam, something that many pre-war households had done. However the fruit was still readily available with raspberries and brambles growing in abundance throughout the district.

Although neither fish nor potatoes was rationed they were not always readily available. The district was well supplied with fish and chip shops and, if the proprietor had enough stock to make it worth his while cooking, the message "Frying Tonight" would appear in the shop window.

Despite the inevitable shortages, rationing worked. Nobody starved and the balance struck by the Government nutritionists meant that the children who grew up in the 1940s under rationing were in general fitter and healthier than any others, before or since.

Of course it was not only food which could be hard to find. Soap, soap powder and toothpaste were also scarce. One method of cleaning your teeth without toothpaste was to use soot! Clothes, blankets and other materials were also in very short supply and many people improvised. Curtains were recycled into dresses and blankets, when they could be found, became coats or dressing gowns. Anyone lucky enough to find a parachute could have silk underwear!

Many furniture makers were required to manufacture wooden components for the aircraft industry, so new furniture was difficult to find. It was possible to buy so called "Utility" furniture, made using lower quality materials than previously, and not quite so well finished. Well made and durable, it is still possible to find "Utility" items on sale second hand today.

The Social Scene

There was always something to do in wartime Falkirk. It was quite possible to be out every night of the week if you so wished, and one of the most popular forms of entertainment was the "pictures". The district was well provided with cinemas and the programme of two films to each house generally changed twice a week. Adverts for "the pictures" from a Falkirk Herald of April 1942 are reproduced on the next page.

The Picture House, Bank Street, Falkirk
Monday to Wednesday
"Ex Champ" starring Victor McLaglen, Tom Brown, Nan Grey
Also
"Border Legion" starring Roy Rogers and Carl Hughes.
Thursday to Saturday
"Dulcy" starring Ann Sothern, Ian Hunter, Billie Burke
Also
"Phantom Light" starring Gordon Harker and Ian Hunter

The Salon Photo Playhouse, Vicar Street, Falkirk
Showing all Week
"Caught in the Draft" starring Bob Hope and Dorothy Lamour
Also
"Border Vigilantes" starring William Boyd

The Regal, Prince's Street, Falkirk (Falkirk's Cinema For Comfort)
Monday to Wednesday
"She Knew All the Answers" starring Joan Bennett and Franchot Tone
Also
"Murder by Invitation" starring Wallace Ford and Marion Marsh
Thursday to Saturday
"Ice-Capades" starring Dorothy Lewis and James Ellison

The Pavilion, Newmarket Street, Falkirk
Showing all Week
"Honkey Tonk" starring Clark Gable and Lana Turner
Also
"Invasion - Dare Hitler Try?" A Film That Affects YOU

The Cinema, Melville Street, Falkirk
Showing all Week
"Unfinished Business" starring Irene Dunn and Robert Montgomery
Also
"Private Nurse" starring Jane Darwell and Brenda Joyce

The Picture House, Brightons
Monday, Tuesday
"Escape to Glory" starring Pat O'Brien and Constance Bennett
Also
"On Special Duty" starring Charles Starrett
Wednesday, Thursday
"Sleepers West" starring Lloyd Nolan and Lynn Bari
Also
"Penn of Pennsylvania" starring Deborah Kerr and Clifford Evans

The Ritz, Camelon
Monday, Tuesday
"Vivacious Lady" starring James Stewart and Ginger Rogers
Also
"Pioneers of the West" starring The Three Mesquiteers
Wednesday, Thursday
"Hells Angels" starring Jean Harlow and Ben Lyon
Also
"Cavalcade Of Variety" starring Billy Cotton, his Band and All-Star Cast
Friday, Saturday
"Lady Scarface" starring Dennis O'Keefe and Frances Neal
Also
"Hurry, Charlie, Hurry" starring Leon Errol and Mildred Coles
Plus Coloured Cartoon - Crazy House

The Picture Palace, Stenhousemuir
Monday, Tuesday
"My Life Is Yours" starring Lew Ayres and Larraine Day
Also
"Burma Convoy" starring Charles Bickford
Wednesday Only
"The Getaway" starring Donna Reed and Robert Sterling
Thursday, Friday, Saturday
"I Thank You "starring Arthur Askey and Richard Murdoch
Also
"Invasion - Dare Hitler Try?" A Film That Affects YOU

Cinema De Luxe, Denny
Monday, Tuesday
"Kitty Foyle" starring Ginger Rogers, Denis Morgan and James Craig
Wednesday, Thursday
"So Ends Our Night" starring Frederic March
Friday, Saturday
"Turned Out Nice Again" starring George Formby

The Picture House, Denny
Monday, Tuesday
"Sign of the Wolf" by Jack London
Also
"South Of Panama" starring Roger Pryor
Wednesday, Thursday
"Facing the Music" starring Bunny Doyle and Betty Driver
Also "Junior G-Men" Final Episode!
Friday, Saturday
"Road Show" starring Adolphe Menjou, Carole Landis and Charles Butterworth

The same edition of the Herald also advertises a Full Variety Show at the Roxy Theatre on Friday and Saturday with two shows each night and a Grand Talent Night also on the Friday. Theatres like the Roxy made good use of local talent for their shows, and this resource was very effectively swelled by the availability of hundreds of locally posted servicemen. The well-known singer and entertainer Max Bygraves had one of his first professional bookings at the Roxy Theatre while serving with the air force in Grangemouth.

The Ice Rink had skating all day Saturday, Wednesday afternoon and every evening except Tuesday. Curling was available all day Tuesday and Thursday afternoon. There was dancing each evening with Joe Gibson and his London Band, except Tuesday evening when there was Scottish dancing with William Hannah and his Band! Children and members of the Armed Forces paid 9d with adults paying 1/6. Regular ice hockey league matches were also a major attraction in the Ice Rink.

If you preferred to be out of doors you could visit Horne's Fun Fair and Carnival in Denny Public Park, where "All the latest Novelties" would be available.

The Spitfire Funds

Many of the social events held during the war years were intended to help raise money for charitable causes, such as the Prisoner of War Relief Fund or the War Relief Fund. However the most successful fund raising activity to take place was probably that aimed at buying a Spitfire for the RAF.

The Falkirk Herald launched its "Spitfire Fund" in the summer of 1940, at the height of the Battle of Britain. The target amount needed to "buy" a Spitfire was £5,000 and the people of the district set about the task with enthusiasm. All manner of events were held to raise money, including a Sale of Work in   Orchard Street, Grangemouth in September 1940 which raised a total of £4 6 shillings. Children from all over the district sold lavender or took part in "Back Court Parade" concert parties, often held in the Roxy Theatre. One such event in November 1940 raised the impressive sum of £17 18s 6d. The fund received a major boost, also in November, when the famous entertainer Sir Harry Lauder topped the bill at a concert in Falkirk Town Hall in Newmarket Street. This concert raised £160. Donations were also received from expatriate "Bairns" from all over the world, particularly the U.S.A.

Towards the end of November 1940, with the fund standing at £2,313, the editor of the Herald was visited by Frank Muirhead of Abbotshaugh House, Bainsford. Mr Muirhead was a successful timber merchant and he wanted to contribute to the cause. He handed the editor a cheque for £5,000, asking only that "his" Spitfire should carry the name "Abbotshaugh Falkirk Bairn".

Mr Muirhead's generous donation was passed to the Air Ministry and work proceeded to raise the £2500 still needed for the "Falkirk Bairn". By October 1940 the Herald was able to report:

"THE BAIRN" ASSURED
We are happy to announce today that the Falkirk Fighter Fund has reached - and surpassed - the £10,000 mark aimed for. Thus there has been brought to Triumphant Consummation the grand effort embarked upon 14 months ago by the people of Falkirk with the object of raising the price of a fighter plane to be named "The Falkirk Bairn".

The final amount raised and passed on to the Air Ministry was £10,120 14s 1d.

Substantial sums of money were raised by Spitfire Funds all over the country, but it is important to note that it was not actually used to "buy" a Spitfire. Contracts for aircraft production were placed by the Government many months in advance and could involve hundreds of individual planes. Most of the money raised was used by the Air Ministry for welfare work.

A Spitfire Fund Concert, Stewart Road, Falkirk
Falkirk Museums Service via the Author

IN THE HOUR OF PERIL
PEOPLE OF FALKIRK
AND DISTRICT
EARNED THE GRATITUDE
OF THE BRITISH NATIONS
SUSTAINING THE VALOUR OF
THE ROYAL AIR FORCE
AND FORTIFYING THE CAUSE
OF FREEDOM
BY THE GIFT OF
SPITFIRE AIRCRAFT

They shall mount up with wings as eagles
Issued by the Ministry of Aircraft Production
1941

The Spitfire Fund plaque, on display in the Falkirk Herald office in Newmarket Street, Falkirk
Falkirk Herald

The efforts of the Spitfire Funds were looked on favourably in official circles because they were seen as a way of encouraging communities to "pull together" towards a common goal. This was reinforced by letting the group or individual that had raised the money name an aircraft already on the production line. This name was painted on the aircraft and entered on its official service record card (Form 78). The fundraisers were also sent a wooden plaque, a photograph of the aircraft displaying its name and a letter of thanks from the Minister of Aircraft Production.

At least two, and possibly three, Spitfires would eventually carry Falkirk names. Other towns around the district also had Spitfire Funds, but a search of production records has so far failed to locate any other Spitfire with a local name.

The first of the Falkirk Spitfires to enter service was "Abbotshaugh Falkirk Bairn", serial no. W3207. This aircraft is described on its record card as an LF (Low Flying) Mk Vb. After its initial period of service with 609 and 222 Squadrons, it was fitted with a newer, more powerful, Rolls Royce Merlin 55 engine and clipped wingtips making it more suitable for low altitude operations before being returned to active service.

This Spitfire went on to serve with 317, 413, 126, 133, 132, 504 and 310 Squadrons before being sent to 61 Operational Training Unit in July 1944. It survived the war to be written off after crashing into a truck while taxiing at Keevil airfield in September 1945.

"The Falkirk Bairn" itself, W3243, was built at Eastleigh as part of the same batch as W3207, against an order originally placed in the summer of 1940. It was the 1,684th Spitfire to be built. It had a much shorter career, serving with 611, 315 and 167 Squadrons, before being lost in an accident on September 19th 1942. Its photograph appeared in the Herald on December 6th 1941.

According to letters sent by the Air Ministry, both Falkirk Spitfires shot down enemy aircraft.

There were other ways to raise money to help in the war effort. The "Wings For Victory" campaign was launched to encourage people to join the National Savings Scheme by illustrating how their savings would be used to help fund purchases of aircraft for the air force. Falkirk Museums Service archive contains a copy of a logbook, apparently from a Short Stirling bomber belonging

"The Falkirk Bairn"
Falkirk Museums Service

to No. 7 Squadron and bought with money invested in the National Savings Scheme by the people of Larbert and Stenhousemuir. These ommunities subscribed a total of over £70,000, apparently enough for the Stirling and six Spitfires.

According to the logbook the Stirling carried the serial number BF390 and took part in many raids against enemy territory, including several visits to Germany and at least one to Italy. The aircraft failed to return from operations over the Berlin area in November 1943.

War Babies

In the late summer of 1939, with war looking more likely, the Government put into effect a scheme to evacuate children from the vulnerable urban areas of Clydeside and find them homes for the duration of hostilities in less dangerous rural areas.

On Friday September 1st 1939, a train pulled into Falkirk High station carrying about 100 children from Glasgow. They assembled on the platform before being led to Falkirk High School (Woodlands) where they were fed and given a bag containing their rations for the next two days. According to the Falkirk Herald, the bag contained one can of corned beef; a large can of milk and a smaller can of sweetened milk; 1 pound of biscuits and ˇ pound of chocolate.

The children then boarded buses which took them to Avonbridge, Limerigg, Slamannan and Muiravonside, where they were to be billeted. They were given sandwiches and a medical check, registered and taken to their new homes. According to the Herald many of these city children found living in the countryside a high adventure. One evacuee was said to be suspicious of cows, but to have struck up an immediate friendship with the farm collie!

For children growing up during the war years there seems to have been a tremendous sense of adventure. School went on as normal although in some cases facilities had to be shared as the military or civil authorities had commandeered buildings. Comely Park School, for example, was used by the army and its pupils were sent to Victoria School in Queen Street. Since there was not enough room to teach them all at once some children attended in the mornings and others in the afternoons.

For very young children, with fathers either in the forces or local industries and mothers perhaps doing war work, special nurseries were built. Falkirk Town Council approved three, located in Arnot Street, Falkirk, Merchiston Avenue, Bainsford and Stirling Road, Camelon. For older children with working parents, dining facilities were opened in the Science and Art School in Park Street where they could get meals even during the school holidays. Toys were in short supply but bikes could still be bought, so cycling was a popular hobby.

The Nursery in Merchiston Avenue, still in use today. Note the disused air raid shelter.
Author

Older children with bikes could join the AFS as messengers. Air raid shelters made good gang huts and there was always the possibility of something out of the ordinary happening. For example, when a Hurricane fighter from Grangemouth airfield crashed at the bottom of David's Loan in the summer of 1940, local children arrived on the scene before the air force crash crew. The Hurricane disintegrated on impact, and bits and pieces were lying all around. A belt of .303 inch machine gun ammunition was "liberated" from the wreck and taken to Dollar Avenue Park. Here the bullets were carefully removed from the cartridges, the cordite charge taken out and used to make firework rockets!

The Italian Community

In common with most other parts of Scotland the district had a large Italian community, many of who had been in the country since the beginning of the century and had raised families here. Many had also established successful businesses.

Although Italy was governed by the fascist dictator Benito Mussolini and had been a military ally of Germany during the Spanish Civil War she did not enter the war in 1939, despite constant appeals from Hitler to do so. However, with the German successes in Europe and a seemingly inevitable victory over Great Britain, Mussolini finally came off the fence in June 1940 and declared war on Britain and her allies. This decision, while perhaps not entirely unexpected, was a blow to the British government which had been working frantically behind the scenes to keep Italy neutral.

The entry of Italy into the war served to increase still further the widespread anxiety over this country's immediate situation, and this anxiety manifested itself in part in attacks on Italian owned property. Police reports from the period tell of windows broken in Italian owned businesses in Falkirk and Bo'ness and persecution of some members of the Italian community.

To make matters still worse thousands of Italians were detained and interned. Some were sent to internment camps on the Isle of Man but others were forced to travel as far as Canada. These deportations led to tragedy when the passenger ship Arandora Star, en route to Canada, was torpedoed by a German submarine in the Atlantic Ocean. Many of the German and Italian deportees on board were drowned in the disaster.

THE MILITARY IN FALKIRK

The evacuees were quickly followed into the district by the armed forces, who requisitioned several buildings for their needs. The air force took over several villas in Bo'ness Road, Grangemouth as well as Grangemouth Town Hall, the Scottish Oils mess room in Oswald Avenue and the new and still unoccupied Westquarter Primary School. In Falkirk the army occupied Rosehall House in the Pleasance, headquarters of the local Scout troop, from July 1940 to November 1942, and apparently used it as accommodation for troops in transit.

The Royal Navy was also active locally. At the outbreak of war naval personnel scoured the coast of the River Forth looking for any ship which could be pressed into service. Even vessels that would need a considerable amount of work to bring them to a useable condition were surveyed. It is said that navy inspectors even examined a ship being broken up at Bo'ness to see if it could be reassembled! Unfortunately, in this case, work had progressed too far to be economically reversed. During the course of hostilities the navy operated refuelling facilities at Grangemouth Docks.

Later in the war the navy also found the large numbers of railway sidings available in the district useful for storing ammunition. Large numbers of railway wagons carrying what must have been vast quantities of shells were parked in sidings around Causewayend and Almond Foundry in Muiravonside, near Whitecross. They were guarded by both Polish and British troops, and there is even a suggestion that some wagons were parked on the Slamannan Railway branch, where they would have been passed every day by passenger trains!

The Home Guard

With a large number of men in reserved occupations throughout the district, there was no shortage of volunteers for the local Home Guard and platoons were established in all local towns and villages, and also in most large factories or other workplaces.

The Home Guard had its origins in a plan published in May 1940 by Anthony Eden, Secretary of State for War, calling for men aged between 17 and 65 who were either in reserved occupations or waiting to go into the armed services to give up some of their time on anti-invasion and anti-parachutist patrols. Volunteers would be uniformed and armed, and at first experience of handling fire-

Grangemouth Home Guard on parade in Lumley Street
Falkirk Museums Service

arms was a necessary qualification for admission. The majority of volunteers were therefore men aged over 40 who had served in the First World War, and in a few cases the Boer War. The Falkirk Herald estimated that more than 200 volunteered in Falkirk alone.

The organisation was known at first as the Local Defence Volunteers (LDV) and the uniform consisted of nothing more than an armband. Weapons were also in short supply as the army gave priority to re-equipping the soldiers who had been evacuated after the fall of France. The LDV commander in East Stirlingshire, Major Alexander Anderson, appealed for shotguns or any other arms to be made available through local police offices to provide a pool of weapons. He also asked for the use of cars and trucks.

Later in 1940 the name of the organisation was changed to the Home Guard, and supplies of uniforms and weapons became slightly more regular. There was one hitch, however, when uniforms meant for the local platoons were commandeered and sent to the Greek army, who were fighting an invasion by Italian, and later German, troops. New uniforms did eventually arrive.

A typical unit was No 13 Platoon, C Company, 2nd Battalion, Stirlingshire Home Guard, based in Slamannan. The platoon came under the control of Company headquarters at the Burgh Stables in High Station Road, Falkirk where the commanding officer was Major John Farrell, who had replaced Major Anderson. Major Farrell would later be the headmaster of St Francis Primary School and a

Town Councillor. The platoon had a notional strength of around 40 men, mostly miners, who gave up one night a week and their weekends, depending on their shifts in the mines, to serve in the Home Guard. At first many of the volunteers were elderly, as portrayed in the television series "Dad's Army", but these gentlemen soon gave way to younger and fitter volunteers from the mines. Their first commander was Lt Ewing, curiously enough the local bank manager, who was later replaced by Lt Kerr, a miner.

The platoon patrolled the area around the village keeping a look out for enemy parachute troops. They were armed with Lee-Enfield rifles, the standard army issue, and the Browning Automatic Rifle, an American light machine gun that was never used in any numbers by the regular army. Weapons training took place in a disused local quarry and at the army shooting range at Greenhill.

Weekend exercises under army instructors occasionally took place at the specialist training ground at Sheriffmuir, where replica pill boxes and strong points had been built. By the end of the war the local Home Guard units were a formidable force, officially categorised just below front line combat troops and higher than many of the regular soldiers who did jobs such as manning searchlights.

The Free Polish Armed Forces

Wartime Falkirk became home to large numbers of Polish servicemen, who had left their country after the German invasion. For many of them the route to Falkirk was long and dangerous. As the German advance from the west was followed a few days later by the Russians invading from the east, many Polish soldiers and civilians fled southwards and over the border into Rumania. From there they travelled through Italy to France to fight with the French army, and when that country fell they made their way to Britain.

A large contingent of Polish soldiers found themselves in French army units pressed against the border of neutral Switzerland. Rather than surrender to the Germans the French commander decided to cross the border, where his troops were interned. Many escaped, however, and made their way through Europe to neutral Portugal, from where they travelled to Britain to join the Free Polish forces. In all some 20,000 servicemen and 3,000 civilians made their way to Britain where they came under the command of General Wladyslaw Sikorski, the Polish Prime Minister and Commander-in-Chief.

The decision was taken to move the Polish soldiers evacuated from France to Central Scotland. As they arrived by ship from France, the soldiers were sent on by train to Glasgow and from there to the various camps established for them. Now known as the First Polish Army Corps they were sent to defend the east coast from Rosyth to Montrose to counter the threat of an invasion of Scotland from occupied Norway.

The headquarters of the First Polish Armoured Division was established at Tulliallan Castle near Kincardine. Its military police and signals units occupied South Bantaskine House while a number of other departments were based at Kinnaird. Soldiers were billeted at the Corporation Street Hostel and officers, in general, stayed in private houses. Falkirk schoolchildren were even taught a few words of Polish to try to make the soldiers feel welcome in what must have been very strange surroundings. The pupils at Victoria Primary School learned the Polish National Anthem and sung it to a delegation that visited the school.

After D-Day the First Polish Armoured Division was deeply involved in the fighting in occupied Europe, particularly the attempt to relieve the besieged Allied paratroops who had landed behind German lines at Arnhem in Holland. The Poles pushed into north western Germany and were present when Field Marshal Montgomery took the German surrender in May 1945.

There were about 250,000 Polish servicemen under arms at the end of the war. Poland herself remained under Russian occupation and Stalin refused to allow the soldiers to return home as an army, only as civilians. Some did, but stories began to reach the remainder of imprisonment and even execution of their comrades, so the majority took up the British government's offer of political asylum. They and their families form a distinctive and important part of the community to this day.

Prisoners of War

During the campaigns in the deserts of Libya and Egypt, the Allied armies took large number of Italian prisoners. They were transported to Britain and housed in specially constructed POW camps. One such was camp No.64 at Castlerankine, near Denny. It seems that the Italian prisoners at Denny were almost universally liked by local people. They went to work in a number of local farms and businesses, including Stein's brickwork at Castlecary. The Italians remained at Denny until they were repatriated after the Italian surrender in

1943 and the site was then used to house German prisoners brought back to Europe from camps in the United States.

The ending of the war in Europe in May 1945 did not see an immediate release of prisoners. They were sent back to Germany in batches, so many remained for several months after hostilities had ceased. In addition a number chose to stay in Scotland rather than return to the devastation of their homeland. Castlerankine's last inmates were transferred to the large POW camp at Comrie in Perthshire in January 1948 and the camp was closed. It was subsequently used as a pig farm, but little remains today.

de Havilland Tiger Moth trainers of No. 35 Elementary & Reserve Flying Training School at Grangemouth Airfield, Summer 1939

Falkirk Museums Service

GRANGEMOUTH AIRFIELD

The most important military site in the Falkirk area was, without doubt, Grangemouth airfield, at the outbreak of war the largest and most modern airfield in Scotland. The airfield's origins lay in the Government's plan, outlined in the first chapter, to be prepared for a war in 1939. Part of this plan called for an increase in the size and training of reserve forces like the Territorial Army, the Royal Navy and the Royal Air Force Volunteer Reserves.

The Government wanted to train more pilots and other aircrew and a new company, Scottish Aviation Limited, was formed to build and run training schools in Scotland. The company opened their west of Scotland flying school at Prestwick, near Ayr, and turned its attention to the outstanding contract for the east of Scotland. After looking at and rejecting existing sites around Edinburgh their attention focused on an area of land lying between the town of Grangemouth and the River Avon. This site had formed the basis of an earlier attempt to develop an airfield to serve Falkirk and Grangemouth in the early 1930s, but nothing had come of the plan. The site was also used for regular summer air shows organised by travelling "flying circuses".

In the first few weeks of 1939 Scottish Aviation Limited purchased 521 acres, including part of the town golf course and the farms of Reddoch, Claret, Wholeflats, Abbotsgrange and part of Bowhouse. On February 7th the company's Contracts Department set about preparing the site but they could only work on a small area at a time, as the Air Ministry wanted the airfield to be available at short notice if the international situation deteriorated suddenly. Construction also began on two large hangars, a central administration block and office accommodation.

Progress was remarkably fast and just over a month after work had started the new Grangemouth airfield saw its first aircraft when an Avro Anson, flown by Flight Lieutenant Johnstone of the City of Glasgow Auxiliary Squadron, arrived to perform the official Air Ministry approach and surface tests.

On May 1st the Reserve Flying School commenced operations. Officially titled 35 Elementary and Reserve Flying Training School, this unit recruited trainee pilots from Edinburgh and the east of Scotland and taught them to fly. The main aircraft used was the Tiger Moth, and although Scottish Aviation Limited was a private company their aircraft were painted in RAF colours of dark green and dark earth camouflage on the upper surfaces and trainer yellow below. They also carried military markings and serial numbers. For more advanced students 35 E&RFTS also operated a few of the more powerful Hawker Hart biplanes and Fairey Battle light bombers.

Within a few weeks another unit began operations. This was No 10 Civilian Air Navigator's School, which complemented the Reserve Flying School by training other aircrew, such as navigators and observers. Their equipment was the Avro Anson twin-engined general-purpose aircraft. Grangemouth was a busy place in the summer of 1939, with the resident aircraft being joined by regular visitors from both the City of Edinburgh and the City of Glasgow Auxiliary Squadrons, and the occasional Fleet Air Arm aircraft from Navy airfields around the River Forth.

War

Prime Minister Chamberlain's declaration of war had a number of immediate effects on the airfield. Civilian aviation came to an end and all civil aircraft and airfields were requisitioned by the Air Ministry. The resident units were broken up quickly as both pupils and instructors were called up and aircraft were allocated elsewhere.

Grangemouth now came under the direction of 13 Group, Fighter Command, reporting to headquarters at RAF Turnhouse (today the site of Edinburgh Airport). Within a few minutes of the Prime Minister's radio broadcast there was an alert in Grangemouth as unidentified aircraft appeared over the town. It soon became apparent that they were in fact friendly as they banked over the airfield and landed on the grass runway. The aircraft were Spitfires belonging to the City of Glasgow Auxiliary Squadron, which had by now adopted its wartime identity of 602 Squadron, led by the same Flight Lieutenant Johnstone who had performed the acceptance trials only four months previously. Grangemouth was to be one of its forward operating bases.

Although Grangemouth was a large airfield there were insufficient buildings to accommodate many people living on the site. To house the numbers of air force personnel who arrived, numerous buildings were requisitioned to serve as barracks including Grangemouth Town Hall and the newly built and yet to be occupied Westquarter Primary School. Even then, however, some airmen had to be content with bell tents and washing and shaving in tin baths!

Aerial photograph of RAF Grangemouth taken by an RAF photographic reconnaissance aircraft in 1943. Bo'ness Road crosses the picture, with the main hangars and the terminal building just above. Over 30 aircraft, mostly Spitfires, can be seen in the original print.

Courtesy of the Royal Commission on the Ancient and Historic Monuments of Scotland

A Fighter Station

Grangemouth became an important base for RAF squadrons converting to new equipment. The first of these was 141 Squadron, which formed at Turnhouse on October 4th 1939. It was initially equipped with Gloster Gladiator biplanes, which were brought to Grangemouth later the same month. The intention was that the squadron would convert to the new Boulton Paul Defiant two-seat fighter but, since these would not be available in sufficient numbers until 1940, a number of Bristol Blenheim twin engined light bombers were supplied. These aircraft were adapted as temporary fighters by fitting packs of four machine guns under the belly. These aircraft allowed pilots and air gunners to develop the skills of working as a team.

In June 1940 141 Squadron, now equipped with their full complement of the new Defiants, left Grangemouth for Turnhouse and on July 11th it moved on to West Malling airfield in the south of England to take part in the rapidly developing Battle of Britain.

In order to fill the air defence gap created by these movements 263 Squadron moved into Grangemouth from Turnhouse in June. This unit had only recently reformed after losing its aircraft in the ill-fated campaign to oppose the German invasion of Norway. 263 brought with it some Hurricane fighters but it too was scheduled to receive new equipment, this time the RAF's secret weapon, the sleek, twin-engined, heavily armed and very fast Westland Whirlwind fighter.

Unfortunately the Whirlwind was plagued by chronic engine defects and only one or two were available at any time, so the vast majority of 263's work had to be done with Hurricanes. However, even this already small number of operational Whirlwinds was reduced when one of them (serial number P6966) suffered a spectacular crash on August 7th.

Pilot Officer McDermott was taking off from Grangemouth on a training flight when one of the tyres burst. Keeping the undercarriage lowered, he flew around the flying control office to allow the squadron's engineering officers to examine the aircraft through binoculars. Their recommendation was that the burst had damaged the undercarriage, making the aircraft dangerous to land, so he should gain as much height as possible, aim the nose at an unoccupied area of land and bail out. Pilot Officer McDermott climbed to 18,000 feet over Dunmore Moss, put the Whirlwind into a dive and jumped out. The aircraft impacted the soft ground and most of the structure broke up, but the guns and engines kept going down into the peat . They were recovered only in the late 1970's! Pilot Officer McDermott landed safely.

Two weeks later, on August 25th, the squadron lost a Hurricane in equally noteworthy circumstances. Pilot Officer Stein was flying over Denny when his engine caught fire. He tried to get back to the airfield but the damage was too severe, so he too bailed out. The Hurricane, unmanned and by now well alight, flew on to Dalderse Farm, at the foot of David's Loan in Bainsford, where it crashed into a ditch. Pilot Officer Stein drifted eastwards on his parachute and eventually came to earth within the boundaries of Grangemouth Docks. He was promptly arrested for unauthorised entry into a restricted area, and was only released when the squadron commander, Squadron Leader Eeles, came along to vouch for his identity! This was the aircraft that contributed the bullets for the firework experiments noted earlier.

Plan "Banquet"

Although Grangemouth spent the summer of 1940 as both a fighter station providing local defence and as a base at which squadrons could familiarise themselves with new equipment, it also featured in a much more sinister role.

On June 8th 614 Squadron arrived at the airfield. It was equipped with Westland Lysander MkII army co-operation aircraft, the same type as would find fame later in the war by dropping and collecting secret agents in occupied Europe. 614's official duty was to patrol the east coast of Scotland, looking for any German attempts to launch an invasion from recently conquered Norway or Denmark. They were also to exercise with locally based army units. However, 614's true role at Grangemouth was highly secret. Its crews were indeed carrying out anti-invasion patrols, but they were equipped to use chemical weapons against any landing.

Following the evacuation of the Allied armies from Dunkirk in May 1940 the Government, and particularly Prime Minister Churchill, believed that the Germans would not stop at the coast of Europe and would attempt an invasion. The British army had left huge quantities of weapons behind it in France and Belgium and it would take time to replace these stocks. In the meantime, desperate measures would be needed to fight any invading force. Under Plan "Banquet", a number of RAF squadrons were, in great secrecy, equipped and trained to spray mustard gas. Mustard gas, as noted in the first chapter, is in fact a liquid rather than a vapour. It causes severe skin irritation, blisters, blindness and burning on contact. It can also affect breathing if it is inhaled. Although it would not necessarily have been fatal to any invaders, it would have required them to wear specialised protective clothing and would have greatly hampered their ability to operate as an effective force. The coast of Scotland was to be covered from both Grangemouth and Lossiemouth, with squadrons based at these airfields sending detachments to outlying sites. 614 Squadron, for example, had forward operating bases at locations as far apart as Montrose and Dumfries.

The Lysander aircraft needed only the very minimum of conversion for their new role. They were already fitted with the necessary equipment to carry chemical smoke tanks for laying smoke screens. The chemical smoke was also stored as a liquid so the tanks needed only minor modification to deal with the more corrosive mustard gas liquid. The gas itself was stored on the airfield and moved around the country in trucks. There was at least one accident involving mustard gas at Grangemouth that resulted in an airman being treated at Falkirk Infirmary.

To learn the techniques of gas spraying 614 Squadron used the facilities at Barry Buddon range, near Carnoustie. Their aircraft carried nothing more lethal than water on these occasions!

Fighter Pilot Training

Throughout the summer of 1940 Grangemouth was extremely busy. Fighter squadrons rotated through the airfield and 614's Lysanders went about their business. The RAF was also occupied in the south of England, fighting the actions remembered today as the Battle of Britain.

Even in the darkest days of the Battle, in August and September 1940, industry kept the air force more than adequately supplied with a constant flow of new aircraft. It was, however, impossible to train pilots quickly enough to keep up with casualties and both the regular and auxiliary fighter squadrons were severely stretched. Pilots were drafted in from other RAF Commands and from the Fleet Air Arm. There were volunteers from neutral countries, like the USA, and experienced Polish and Czech pilots with only a limited command of English and little experience of RAF fighter aircraft. They were all thrown into the fighting.

**A fine study of a Spitfire Mk1 of No. 58 OTU parked in front of the hangars at
Grangemouth some time in early 1941.**
Falkirk Museums Service via the Author

The Air Ministry was determined that this situation would never arise again.
With the Battle of Britain at its height plans were laid for a greatly expanded
pilot training system. Numerous airfields in areas away from the front line were
selected to house new Operational Training Units. One such was Grangemouth,
chosen to house 58 OTU, part of 81 (Training) Group of Fighter Command.

Although the OTU was originally intended to open in October 1940 for the
training of night fighter crews this was quickly changed to the training of Spitfire pilots. The OTU eventually formed at Grangemouth on December 2nd 1940.
Its task was to take newly qualified pilots and teach them to fly and fight in
Spitfires, of which they had only a handful at that time.

To accommodate the new training school a massive programme of building
work began at the airfield. Two new tarmac runways replaced the old grass
flying field. The runways were connected by a perimeter track, off which were
built dispersal areas and taxiways. New offices, barracks, workshops and hangars were also built. A new site was also developed on the other side of the
Bo'ness Road to house lecture and flight simulator facilities.

Another aerial photograph of the airfield from the 1943 set, this time showing part of the perimeter track and the dispersal areas. The River Avon is in the top left hand corner. Once again many Spitfires can be seen in the original print.
Courtesy of the Royal Commission on the Ancient and Historic Monuments of Scotland

A few weeks after the formation of the training school Grangemouth was visited by HRH Group Captain the Duke of Kent, who was serving as a Fighter Command Welfare Officer. By all accounts he was impressed by what he saw, as the school was now ready for its first intake of students. The trainee pilots would have arrived in the midst of the building work but at least there were aircraft for them to fly, as more Spitfires arrived, the majority of them veterans of the Battle of Britain, now replaced in front line squadrons by later marks. Many of these aircraft had been damaged in combat or accidents and subsequently repaired, adding to the stresses combat had already imposed on their airframes. Some of these Spitfires were damaged in landing accidents, which resulted in an extension to the main runway being built.

Other aircraft were required as well. The new pilots would have learned to fly on aircraft such as the Tiger Moth biplane and the first stage of their training was to introduce them to something more powerful. At Grangemouth this was the Miles Master two-seat advanced trainer, which accommodated the student pilot in the front cockpit, laid out in the same manner as a contemporary fighter cockpit, and an instructor with dual controls seated to the rear. The Master could also be fitted with a forward firing machine gun and practice bomb carriers for basic weapons training.

Once the instructor was satisfied with his student's progress he would be allowed to "go solo" on the Master before being converted to the Spitfire. There were, at that time, no dual control Spitfires so the instructor would have to be very confident of the student's capabilities before he was allowed to proceed.

After successfully completing his basic training on the Spitfire the student would then be taught aerial gunnery and current air force tactics. Air-to-air marksmanship was practised over the Firth of Forth, with specially marked Fairey Battle, and later Lysander, aircraft towing fabric target banners up and down a set track while the trainees tried to hit them. The ammunition they used had coloured paint in the tip, so each student could assess his own accuracy. It was not unknown for the Battle and Lysander target tugs to return to Grangemouth with bullet holes in them instead of the targets!

Many famous pilots served at Grangemouth, either as students or instructors. It was RAF practice to "rest" front line pilots between tours of duty by posting them as instructors at operational training units. Some of these experienced pilots claimed that dealing with the students was every bit as stressful as combat! Perhaps the most famous ex-Grangemouth pilot was Neville Duke. He arrived as a student in February 1941 and after training joined 92 Squadron, which was then in the process of moving to the Mediterranean. Duke became Grangemouth's first "ace", with a score of five kills, and ended the war with a Distinguished Flying Cross and two bars, the Distinguished Service Order and the Air Force Cross. After the war he would add a world air speed record and OBE to this impressive tally.

Pilots came to Grangemouth from all corners of the earth. There are records of American, Australian, Belgian, Canadian, Czech, Danish, Dutch, Norwegian, Southern Rhodesian and, of course, Polish trainees at Grangemouth. Grangemouth is rightly associated with the Free Polish contingent in the RAF, and from October 1942 all Polish trainee pilots destined for Spitfires were taught at Grangemouth, where Polish instructors served with their British counterparts.

Having mastered the basics, the trainee pilots were then taught fighter tactics. They would practice escorting simulated bomber raids on military, naval and civil targets, with Masters acting as the bombers. They would also dogfight their instructors, who flew specially marked Spitfires known as "jumpers". These Spitfires were probably painted to resemble German fighters, but not too closely! It seems they usually had their noses and propeller spinners painted yellow, white or red.

As well as the regular equipment of the OTU, other aircraft would be seen at Grangemouth. The Air Transport Auxiliary kept a Dragon Rapide airliner belonging to 4 Aircraft Delivery Flight for transporting ferry crews around the country and 58 OTU themselves had a couple of Gloster Gladiator biplane fighters which were used for both aerobatic training and meteorological observation. Operational aircraft and aircraft from other training units were also regular visitors, such as the Swordfish torpedo bombers from the Royal Navy air station at Donibristle, near Rosyth.

The ATA's Dragon Rapide and the OTU's Dominie proved to be particularly popular with the ATC, taking parties of air cadets for "air experience flights" around the district on many occasions.

Grangemouth became so busy that a satellite airfield had to be built to deal with the congestion. This new airfield was built on farmland at Balado Bridge, near Kinross. Balado became the main location for aerial gunnery, leaving Grangemouth free to concentrate on the initial training and conversion. Engineering and administrative functions remained at the parent airfield.

The complement of aircraft also changed. As the new Mk V Spitfire began to appear in front line squadrons the earlier Mk II was made available to training units, replacing the battle weary Mk I's. Curiously, some of Grangemouth's Spitfire Mk I's were taken from the airfield and shipped to Port Sudan in North Africa. What happened to them after that is something of a mystery. The Lysander target tugs were also flown away and replaced by the more powerful Miles Martinet, a derivative of the Master trainer.

Grangemouth and Balado Bridge were extremely busy airfields, which were used by inexperienced pilots flying, in some cases, over stressed aircraft. Accidents were frequent and the loss of aircraft was common. Over the course of its existence 58 OTU lost around 90 Spitfires, 25% of all Spitfires lost over Scotland or in Scottish waters during the war. Some have never been found. For example, Spitfire L1083 was last seen on November 11th 1941 flying into cloud. It simply vanished. In January 1943 three Spitfires flew into Kingseat Hill in the Ochil Hills. Two of the pilots were killed outright, the third was found seriously injured and still in his cockpit by a passing shepherd.

At least one Grangemouth Spitfire is in Loch Lomond and another is in the Lake of Menteith. Other types also crashed. One notable accident occurred just outside Stenhousemuir when a low-flying Master failed to clear rising ground. This aircraft was carrying a Norwegian student and a Polish instructor. Many of these pilots were killed and a number of them are buried in the Air Force plot at Grandsable cemetery, between Grangemouth and Polmont.

The training scheme introduced in 1940 was highly successful and by the middle of 1943 the supply of fighter pilots was outstripping the demand. 58 OTU was given a new role and a new designation, 2 Tactical Exercise Unit. Its new job was to take trained pilots and keep their skills honed through the use of flying and tactical exercises until they were posted to operational squadrons. As well as the resident Spitfires, 2 TEU also operated Hurricane fighters of various types before closing in June 1944.

The closure of 2 TEU marked the end of wartime flying at Grangemouth, but not the end of its wartime role. The airfield became an enormous storage depot for everything from aircraft parts to boots. Some of the buildings emained in use as engineering workshops, in particular for the maintenance crews servicing radar stations along the east coast.

In general, however, the airfield quickly ran down. It saw some operational use and some private flying after the war, but was officially closed in 1955.

THE WHEELS OF INDUSTRY

The Falkirk area contributed much to the success of the Allied cause in the Second World War but the most significant single factor was the output of local industry. During the First World War foundries around the district produced millions of shells, grenades and bombs. This pattern would be repeated in the Second World War, but by then other industries were coming to the fore and their contributions would be equally, if not more, important. Indeed some of the most important elements in the Allied victory were produced in Grangemouth. These were not weapons, however, but drugs.

Medicinal and Other Chemicals

In 1919 Morton Sundour Dyes Ltd acquired land in Grangemouth to build a dyestuffs factory. This was an area in which British industry had been sadly lacking before the First World War when most dyes were bought from Germany. This was obviously impossible during the period of hostilities and immediately afterwards, so Sir James Morton was aiming to plug an obvious gap in the market. By the early 1920s Scottish Dyes Ltd, as the new concern was known, established itself in the chemical manufacture of dyes and in 1926 it amalgamated with the British Dyestuffs Corporation. The new company retained the Scottish Dyes name for another two years, when BDC became one of the four founders of Imperial Chemical Industries Ltd. ICI Grangemouth continued to concentrate on the manufacture of dyestuffs and many important discoveries were made at the site.

In December 1941 the Japanese attacked the American Navy at Pearl Harbour in Hawaii and simultaneously declared war on Britain. Their forces advanced quickly through south-east Asia, in the process overrunning the areas that produced quinine, a drug needed to fight the tropical disease malaria. In order to allow troops to fight effectively in the mosquito-infested jungles of south-east Asia the need for a man made alternative to quinine became urgent. In response ICI chemists developed a substance called "Mepacrine". Mepacrine proved to be highly effective and was put into production at Grangemouth in 1942, the site eventually producing millions of tablets. Later in the war even more effective anti-malarial drugs were manufactured at Grangemouth.

A Luftwaffe photograph of Nobels Explosives Works in Redding in September 1940.
The Union Canal can be seen running across the middle of the photograph, with the main Edinburgh-Glasgow railway line just above.
Courtesy of the Royal Commission on the Ancient and Historic Monuments of Scotland

Because of these discoveries Allied soldiers could move and fight in jungle areas without fear of contracting the disease. The Japanese, who did not have such an effective treatment and generally had more basic medical facilities in any case, often had a larger proportion of their soldiers sick than fit. Mepacrine did have one unfortunate side effect for the Grangemouth process workers; it turned their skin bright yellow!

Mepacrine was vital but other Grangemouth products were almost as important. These were sulpha antibiotics and Cetavlon antiseptics. In the First World War as many as half the Allied soldiers who died actually survived their initial wound, only to succumb to subsequent infection. Even if the infection was detected in time antiseptics were in short supply and the only available treatment was usually amputation of the infected limb. This was one of the motivations that led to research into antibiotics in the period between the Wars, which culminated in Sir Alexander Fleming's isolation of penicillin in 1928. Penicillin was first used in 1941, by which time the search had begun for man- made variants which would lend themselves to large scale manufacture. These were the sulpha drugs.

These drugs greatly reduced the numbers of Allied fatalities by giving wounded soldiers a much better chance of survival. By the middle years of the war antibiotics were also becoming available to the civillian population, with the first recorded use of penicillin in Falkirk Infirmary being in August 1943.

Grangemouth was not the only ICI facility in the district. The company's Nobel division also owned and operated an explosives factory known as ICI Westquarter. This large facility was located on the banks of the Union Canal between Hallglen and Redding, next door to Redding Pit, and specialised in the manufacture of detonators for explosives. The factory had originally been established to manufacture chemical detonators for the mining and quarrying industries. These used fulminate of mercury, an unstable compound which would detonate on impact. It had to be treated extremely carefully and because of its inherent dangers the various buildings at the factory were surrounded by high earth blast walls to contain any accidental explosions.

An important part of ICI Westquarter's wartime contribution was the work done at the site on the electrical detonation of explosives. With unstable chemicals no longer required as detonators the transport and handling of explosives was very much safer and allowed the new generation of high explosives then in use to be more easily controlled.

There were a number of other chemical companies in the area who were also involved in manufacturing for the war effort. Scottish Tar Distillers in Camelon produced a range of chemicals, probably the most important of which was toluene, a key ingredient in the manufacture of explosives. Glycerine, an important constituent of toluene, was supplied by the Co-operative Soap Works in Grangemouth. The soap works also continued to manufacture soap, mostly for the Government, and subsequently lost many of their commercial contracts.

Curiously one industry which did not feature at all in the district's wartime economy was the manufacture of petroleum products. There was a small refinery at Grangemouth before the war, but since its raw material was imported crude oil, and this was in very short supply, it was decommissioned for the duration of hostilities.

Working with Fire and Steel

Several local foundries were given Government contracts to manufacture munitions. In many cases this involved the installation of new machinery or, as in the case of Carron Company the establishment of a dedicated factory, for which Government grants were available. The range of munitions manufactured by local foundries was vast. Carron alone produced around 6 million 25-pound artillery shells, while their former electric cooker shop was converted to manufacture hand grenades. To this production must be added that of the other large manufacturers like Falkirk Iron Co, and the dozens of smaller concerns. Although shell and grenade cases were manufactured in and around Falkirk, they were not filled with their explosive contents here. The majority of these items were taken to Royal Ordnance factories or contractors to be filled.

Government contracts involved more than munitions. As new military bases and airfields were built, and existing facilities expanded, local foundries supplied heating stoves, water boilers, catering equipment and pipework. These products accompanied British or Allied forces around the world, from the deserts of North Africa to India and the jungles of south-east Asia. Existing equipment also had to be maintained or repaired by the manufacturer's staff. Thus many Carron fitters found themselves sent to repair or replace equipment on ships which had been damaged at sea.

The First World War was fought in an era when mechanised road transport and aviation were in their infancy. Most battlefield transportation was provided by either men or horses. Indeed the typical First World War battlefield would have been quite impassable to most mechanised vehicles of the period. The mechanised nature of the war placed new demands on the local foundries. Their expertise was called upon by vehicle, aircraft and ship builders to supply the precision components that these industries required.

Once again the range of products was extremely diverse. The engineering shops in a number of local foundries acted as sub-contractors to aircraft manufacturers, making both cast and fabricated components to be delivered to the central production lines of the major aircraft companies, such as Armstrong-Whitworth, Hawkers, Supermarine and Avro. The same applied to aero engine manufacturers like Bristols and Rolls Royce.

Many other important items were made in local foundries. Carron cast steel tank track links and other mechanical parts. Jones & Campbell made catapult slugs for Royal Navy aircraft carriers. These castings were fitted into the steam catapult on the carrier's deck. Hooks on the aircraft to be launched were attached to these slugs by means of special strops. High pressure steam was released into the catapult barrel, firing the slug along it and accelerating the towed aircraft to take-off speed. At the end of the catapult the slug and the strops fell into the sea. Since each large aircraft carrier had at least three catapults, demand was high. At least one local foundry also manufactured air raid shelters.

Munitions workers at Carron
Falkirk Museums Service

A number of problems affected the foundry industry during the war years. First was a lack of experienced workers, made worse as men either volunteered or were conscripted into the armed forces. Many occupations vital to war work were reserved, and people with these skills were exempt from military service. There remained, however, a serious shortfall at the semi-skilled and unskilled level.

This was a consequence of the slump the industry had suffered in the 1930s, when many skilled men had been laid off. Many of these foundrymen, either unemployed or working in less skilled occupations, were liable to conscription and were called up. Their skills were thus lost to the industry. Once again, as in the First World War, thousands of women were brought into the foundries at the semi-skilled and manual levels to bridge at least part of the gap. The foundries, and other industries, were not immune from industrial action simply because there was a war on. Strikes did happen, with even the mighty Carron Company being forced to reach a settlement with its workforce in a dispute over pay.

A second problem was a lack of high-grade iron ore. This had been imported before the war, particularly from the Scandinavian countries. This trade was halted by the German occupation of Norway and Denmark, forcing the foundries to use lower quality domestic ores for their production.

The other raw material, apart from iron ore, needed by the foundries was coal. At that time the Falkirk area was still a substantial coal producer and miners were "reserved" like skilled ironworkers, and exempt from military service. However manpower shortages still existed and to relieve these a scheme was proposed under which able-bodied men could volunteer to work in the mines rather than join the armed forces. These "Bevin Boys" as they were called, after the Minister of Labour, were recruited from all over the country and sent to coal producing areas. In Falkirk a special camp was built on the Bog Road near Laurieston to accommodate them.

Major investment by the Government saw the introduction of new metal-working technologies when a large aluminium rolling mill was opened in Bainsford in 1943. The location was chosen because of its good transport links and the availability of skilled metal workers. The fact that the local MP, Tom Johnstone, was then the Secretary of State for Scotland may also have had some bearing on the decision!

The mill was operated by the British Aluminium Company and was considered the most modern of its type. Compared to BA's existing rolling mills the Bainsford plant was much more highly mechanised and consequently had a smaller workforce. The mills could take large aluminium blocks up to 2 ° tons in weight and roll them to produce sheets and strips only a few millimetres thick. The vast majority of the aluminium sheet produced during the war years was specialised heat-treated alloy for aircraft manufacture. This accounted for some 75% of all the plant's output.

Shipbuilding

Both Grangemouth and Bo'ness had shipbuilding and repair facilities, while Bo'ness also had shipbreaking yards. These facilities were pressed into service and either manufactured or refitted a large number of ships.

Grangemouth Dockyard Company worked mostly on transport ships, but also built and repaired warships. Thirty-seven ships, with a total tonnage of 53,000 tons, were built and launched from the yard. Thirty-four of these were cargo ships, mostly diesel coasters or small tankers, and three were corvettes for the Royal Navy. One of these, HMS Celandine, which was launched in 1940, was credited with the sinking of the German submarine U-556 on 27 June 1941.

The Dockyard Company also repaired warships, most notably the submarines of the Royal Dutch Navy, which had escaped when Holland was occupied by the Germans in 1940. The Dockyard Company received an official letter of thanks for its work from the Dutch Government after the war. It also converted Royal Navy destroyers for long-range convoy escort duties. One of these, HMS Versatile, was a World War One vintage V class destroyer, which would appear to have been extensively refitted. Another, HMS Shikari, was a more modern design.

The workforce at the yard obviously took a great deal of pride in their work. Nothing illustrates this better than a photograph of one of their ships, the oil tanker SS Empire Trotwood, built in 1944 and launched with a placard attached to her railing which read "Another One From The Grangemouth Dock yard Company Ltd!"

HMS Celandine at Grangemouth, 1940
Falkirk Museums Service

More numerous than the ships built at Grangemouth were those brought in for refit or to have battle damage repaired. The tanker Danmark is one example. She was severely damaged by enemy action and to repair her the Dockyard Company cut her in half and grafted a new stern on to the undamaged bows. The Danmark was returned to service as an oil depot ship at Scapa Flow naval base in the Orkneys, where she was used to refuel destroyers and light cruisers.

Another merchant ship, the Berganza, was brought to Grangemouth with serious damage to her bow. The Dockyard Company was keen to avoid having to dry-dock the ship to carry out repairs. Instead they flooded her aft holds, which lifted her bow out of the water and allowed the work to proceed.

The yards in Bo'ness were also kept busy throughout the war. As well as making sheds for the army, they built wooden-hulled motor torpedo boats of the type used for coastal patrol by the Royal Navy. The Bo'ness yards have one additional claim to fame. At the end of the war the German navy, the Kreigsmarine, was ordered to surrender its submarines and sail them into Highland sea lochs. From there a number of these U-boats were then brought to Bridgeness, where they were broken up. Local legend states that there is one still there, sunk in the mud on the harbour floor!

The Timber Trade

Both Grangemouth and Bo'ness had been major timber importing centres before the war and their woodyards and sawmills were put to good use producing a wide range of goods. Much of the pre-war timber trade had been carried out with the Scandinavian countries but, with Germany occupying both Denmark and Norway, the trade dried up shortly after war was declared. Alternative, domestic, sources of supply had to be found and much of this wood was converted into pit props for the mining industry.

Later in the war, when plans were well advanced for the invasion of continental Europe, they manufactured components for temporary docks and quays, which allowed the Allied forces to offload supplies quickly without the risk and danger involved in capturing a conventional port. The yards also manufactured prefabricated airfield surfaces to allow the operation of close support aircraft from temporary strips as near the front line as possible.

Staff from James Jones in Larbert transporting timber from plantations in the Borders to England. This photograph was taken in The Square, Hawick.
Falkirk Museums Service

Transport

The many and varied products of local industry had to be transported to their destinations and most travelled by rail. Passenger railway services were curtailed to allow as much freight movement as possible and all major manufacturing sites had their own sidings. In the days before the nationalisation of Britain's railways, local freight and passenger services were operated by either London, Midland and Scottish Railways or London and North Eastern Railways. The smart pre-war LMS maroon and LNER apple green liveries on these companies engines were gone, however, to be replaced by a coat of "austerity" black paint, which was much easier to maintain.

The other important transport sites were Grangemouth and Bo'ness Docks, which were very busy throughout the course of the war. Both docks became restricted areas with access by pass only. Shipping in the Forth was a risky business, with the constant threat of mines or air attack. Several vessels sailing to or from Grangemouth were lost to mines or attack by U-boats. One such was the steamship Gasray which was travelling from Grangemouth to Blyth in Northumberland when she was torpedoed by a submarine two miles off St Abbs Head on April 5th 1945, in the last month of the war in Europe.

VICTORY!

O n Tuesday 8th of May 1945 the war in Europe came to an end. The German government had surrendered the day before and the 8th was declared a public holiday. Most churches throughout the district held services of thanksgiving and bells sounded the length and breadth of the country.

Throughout the day a carnival atmosphere prevailed, and as darkness began to fall in Falkirk the crowds made their way to the Burgh Buildings in Newmarket Street. The building had been decked with coloured lights, which were switched on at 10.30pm. For the first time in nearly six years the town also enjoyed the benefit of full street lighting. The Falkirk Herald was moved to comment that a child would have to be over 10 years of age to recall such brightness. For those who preferred to be indoors, there was a Great Victory Dance in the Ice Rink.

In Grangemouth over 700 people, including the Council and Magistrates, attended a service of thanksgiving at Charing Cross church. Later in the evening the town was described as "haywire" as large crowds gathered at Charing Cross. There was dancing and fireworks, and as darkness fell huge bonfires were lit all around the town and the Municipal Chambers were floodlit.

"Welcome Home", Falkirk, 1945
Falkirk Museums Service

In Larbert there were also services of thanksgiving, followed by a victory concert and dance in the Dobbie Hall. The service was led by Mr H W Evans of the Pentecostal Church and the Rev Walter Gordon of Larbert Old Parish. Throughout the district fireworks and bonfires were lit, people danced in the streets and remembered the fallen. The Herald notes that the Wednesday following the festivities was a very quiet day!

However, there was still the matter of the war against Japan. This was brought to an abrupt end by the American use of atomic weapons against Hiroshima and Nagasaki and the subsequent Japanese surrender in early August. The services, parties and bonfires started all over again, and there was a general feeling of a fresh start. This was not only because of the ending of the war. There had been a General Election, known as the "khaki election" because of the number of voters still in the armed forces, which returned Clement Atlee's Labour Party with a large majority. To many people, this was a sure sign of better times to come.

Surrendered U-boats await the cutting torch, Bridgeness
Falkirk Museums Service

ABBREVIATIONS USED

AFS	Auxiliary Fire Service
ARP	Air Raid Precautions
ATA	Air Transport Auxiliary
ATC	Air Training Corps
ATS	Auxiliary Territorial Service
BA	British Aluminium Ltd
BP	British Petroleum Ltd
CANS	Civilian Air Navigators School
E&RFTS	Elementary & Reserve Flying Training School
ICI	Imperial Chemical Industries Ltd
LDV	Local Defence Volunteers (later the Home Guard)
LMS	London, Midland and Scottish Railway
LNER	London and North Eastern Railway
OBE	Order of the British Empire
OTU	Operational Training Unit
POW	Prisoner of War
RAF	Royal Air Force
TEU	Tactical Exercise Unit

VADVoluntary Aid Detachment

SOURCES & GUIDE TO SUGGESTED FURTHER READING

Jefford, C G : **RAF Squadrons**, Airlife, 1988, ISBN 1853100536

Jeffrey, Andrew : **This Present Emergency : Edinburgh, The River Forth and the South Eastof Scotland in the Second World War**, Mainstream, 1992, ISBN 1851585060

Porteous, Robert : **Grangemouth's Modern History**, 2nd rev edn, Falkirk District Libraries, 1994, ISBN 0906586739

Scott, Ian : **The Life & Times of Falkirk**, John Donald, 1994, ISBN 0859763682

Shacklady, Edward & Morgan, Eric : **Spitfire, The History**, Key Publishing, 1988, ISBN 0946219109

Smith, David J : **Action Stations 7, The Military Airfields of Scotland, The North and Northern Ireland**, 2nd edn, Patrick Stephens, 1989, ISBN 1852603097

Sour Milk and Ginger Beer, : Worker's Educational Association, 1987

Sturtivant, Ray : **Royal Air Force Flying Training and Support Units**, Air Britain, 1998, ISBN 0851302521

Walker, John : "Grangemouth Airfield" in **Calatria**, Vol 5, 1993

Walker, John : "Falkirk at War" in **Calatria**, Vol 10, 1996

Watters, Brian : **Where Iron Runs Like Water! A New History of Carron Iron Works 1759-1982**, John Donald, 1998, ISBN 0859765059

Periodicals

Falkirk Herald	:	Various Articles, 1938 - 1945
Calatria	:	The Journal of Falkirk Local History Society : 13 Volumes
Air International	:	Various articles 1980 - date

INDEX

Dawson Park School 17
Denny 39,45
Denny fire brigade 15
Dobbie Hall, Larbert 63
Dollar Avenue Park, Bainsford 34
Donibristle airfield 51
Drem airfield 19
Duke, Sqdn Ldr Neville 50
Dunmore Moss 45

E
Edinburgh 6,19,21
evacuees 32-33
Evans, H.W., Pentecostal Church,
  Larbert 64
Ewing, Lt, Home Guard 37

F
Falkirk Bairn (Spitfire) 29,31
Falkirk Burgh Buildings 63
Falkirk fire brigade 14
Falkirk Football Club 9
Falkirk Herald 9,11,20,26,28,
  32,36,63
Falkirk High School 13,25,32
Falkirk Ice Rink 28,63
Falkirk Infirmary 17,46,55
Falkirk Iron Company 56
Falkirk Science and Art School 33
Falkirk Technical School 9
Falkirk Town Council 8,10,14,33
Falkirk Town Hall 28
Farrell, Maj John, Home Guard
  36-37
fire precautions 14-16
Forth, River 8,18,19,20,35,42
Forth and Clyde Canal 8,15
foundries 7,15,56-58

G
gas 8,11-14,22,46
Gordon, Rev Walter, Larbert Old
  Parish Church 64
Grandsable cemetery 51
Grangemouth airfield 7, 41-52
Grangemouth docks 7,8,20,35,45,62
Grangemouth Dockyard Company
  59-60
Grangemouth Municipal Chambers 64
Greenhill 37
Gumpertz, Miss M.C., cookery
  demonstrator 25

H
Hallglen 55
High Bonnybridge 21
High Station Road, Falkirk 36
Home Guard 35-37

I
ICI Grangemouth 53,55
ICI Westquarter 55-56
Italian community 34

J
Johnston, Tom, MP 59
Jones & Campbell Ltd 57
Jones, James & Sons Ltd 61

K
Kent, Duke of 49
Kerr, Lt, Home Guard 37
Kinnaird 38

L
Larbert 32
Lauder, Sir Harry 28
Lime Street, Grangemouth 15
Limerigg 32

Spitfire Fund 28-32
Stein, John G & Co 39
Stenhousemuir 32,51
Stevenson, John, Royal Marines 6
Stirling County Council 9,10
Stirling District Mental Hospital 17
Stirling Road, Camelon 33
Storp, Lt Sigmund, Luftwaffe 19
sulpha antibiotics 55

T
theatres 9,28
timber trade 61-62
Trenchard, Viscount Hugh 7
Turnhouse airfield 19,42,44

U
U-boats 61,62
Union Canal 8,45,55
Utility furniture 26

V
Victoria School 33,38

W
War Relief Fund 28
Weir Street, Falkirk 13
West Bridge Street, Falkirk 13
Westquarter Primary School 35,44
Whitecross 35
Wholeflats Farm, Grangemouth 41
Wilcock, Ellis, Royal Navy 6
Wings for Victory campaign 31